WHO LIVES NEAR A GLACIER?

Alaska Animals in the Wild

Susi Gregg Fowler

ILLUSTRATED BY **Jim Fowler**

little bigfoot
an imprint of sasquatch books
seattle, wa

Who Lives near a Glacier?

Not much makes its home
on glaciers, I know,
but *near* them you find
more than just ice and snow.
What you see varies
with each glacier you visit,
but it all can be thrilling,
surprising, exquisite.
Creatures and features
to observe and to treasure.
The joy of surprise,
a shiver of pleasure.
A prickly porcupine
lumping along.

A beaver sliding
into a pond.
A seal on an iceberg.
A puffin in flight.
The loon's haunting cry
enchanting the night.
A goat on a rock.
A moose on the shore.
A dragonfly, squirrel,
a salmon, and more.
From forest to stream,
from the air to the ground—
who lives near a glacier?
Just look around!

Alaska has more glaciers than any other state. Scientists estimate the total area of glaciers in Alaska to be 34,000 square miles. That's a lot of ice!

Moose can eat 50 to 60 pounds of food a day, and their stomachs hold as much as 112 pounds at a time. Adult female moose in Alaska weigh up to 1,200 pounds and males up to 1,600 pounds.

Moose

The moose does not apologize
for being of a grander size.
If ranking the world's largest deer,
Alaska moose win, free and clear.

Who'd believe a beast so giant
would have a diet so reliant
on twigs and leaves, sedges, weeds,
to get the food its body needs.

Imagine how much grass and stuff
like weeds it takes to be enough
to fill a beast that big and tall!
They eat, eat, eat from spring to fall.

When winter comes, the moose lose weight—
there's little food on Nature's plate—
but come the spring, they can begin
to fill their bellies up again.

Mountain Goats

It is tricky, you'll admit,
this scramble over stone,
but, sure of foot, I cross with ease—
a talent of my own.

My hooves are made for travel
on slippery, steep terrain.
I leap from ledge to granite cracks,
then jump right back again.

I skip on ridges and moss that clings
to rain-slick planes of rock.
It's nothing for me—I dance across
where you won't even walk.

You'll know me by my sharp black horns
and by my shaggy coat.
I am the queen of the mountain.
I am the mountain goat!

Sure-footed mountain goats depend on cool, high, rocky terrain for survival. Cliffs and ridges around glaciers discourage most predators but pose no problem for mountain goats.

Voles

Eek! Squeak!
Scurry. Streak.
From lakeside up
to mountain peak.
Voles!

Fuzzy coats
and tiny tails,
zipping quickly
up the trails.
Voles!

Most creatures treat
these beasts as food.
They hurry so
they don't get chewed.
Voles!

Eek! Squeak!
Scurry. Streak.
From lakeside up
to mountain peak.
Voles!

Voles are the primary food source for many small mammals and birds in Alaska. Large mammals, like bears and wolves, eat them too. Even fish eat them!

Salmon

They swim and splash,
and then they pause.
Bad idea!
See those jaws?
The hungry bears
come wading in,
so off the salmon
go again.

Splash and slap,
thrash and swish,
salmon are
determined fish.

Below the falls,
they rest in pools—
but not for long,
for instinct rules.
They swim for home.
They carry on.
They have one task:
that is, to spawn.

Mature salmon return from the Pacific Ocean to the freshwater streams and rivers where they hatched, journeying upstream—and even up waterfalls—to spawn.

Both black bears and brown bears are found near streams and on trails around glaciers and throughout much of Alaska.

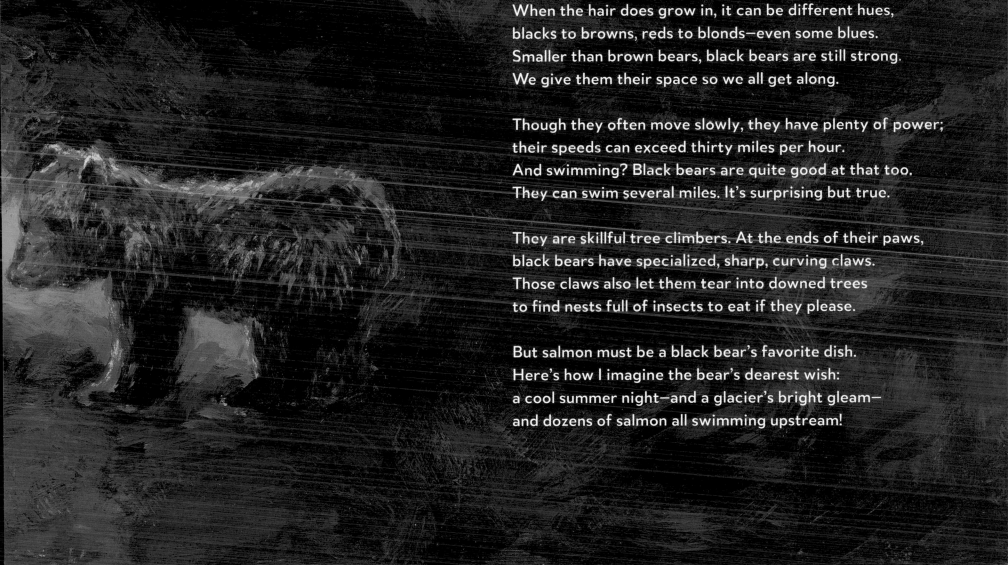

When the hair does grow in, it can be different hues,
blacks to browns, reds to blonds—even some blues.
Smaller than brown bears, black bears are still strong.
We give them their space so we all get along.

Though they often move slowly, they have plenty of power;
their speeds can exceed thirty miles per hour.
And swimming? Black bears are quite good at that too.
They can swim several miles. It's surprising but true.

They are skillful tree climbers. At the ends of their paws,
black bears have specialized, sharp, curving claws.
Those claws also let them tear into downed trees
to find nests full of insects to eat if they please.

But salmon must be a black bear's favorite dish.
Here's how I imagine the bear's dearest wish:
a cool summer night—and a glacier's bright gleam—
and dozens of salmon all swimming upstream!

Harbor Seals

Harbor seal pups in a glacial fjord
are much too adorable to be ignored.
Minutes from birth, the seal pups can swim.
They haul out on icebergs and then jump back in.
Poking out of the water, their little round heads
announce the appearance of these young pinnipeds.
They're playful and curious—it seems sometimes, too,
while you're looking at them, they are looking at you.

Harbor seals often pup in glacial fjords. The classification pinnipeds includes
seals, sea lions, and walrus. The name is derived from Latin pinna for feather
or wing, and pedis for foot—feather-footed or winged feet.

Arctic Terns

To see them, you would never know
just how far
these birds can go.

Ten thousand miles and then return.
Who flies so far?
The arctic tern.

They lift their wings and off they fly,
like tiny angels
in the sky.

They are so small, it's a surprise
that these birds win
the distance prize.

An important lesson: be advised,
you can't judge strength
by someone's size!

Each year arctic terns fly up to 25,000 miles from Antarctica to their arctic breeding grounds and back. They may fly 1.5 million miles during their lifetime—three round trips from Earth to the moon!

Tufted Puffins

If you take a look at seabirds near the shore or out at sea,
you will not find a single bird quite as fine as me.
In summertime, my webbed feet flame red-orange as I fly,
and the feathered tufts along my head flash yellow in the sky.
My bill looks best in summer too—it's colorful and bold,
its winter drab transformed into a brilliant orange and gold.
Whether flying in the sky or swimming in the bay,
I'm about as handsome as they get, so it bugs me when they say
"Clown of the Sea" should be my name. I think, seriously,
they are probably just jealous because they don't look like me!

Tufted puffins and horned puffins spend most of their lives on
the open sea but return to breed on land, often on coastlines
along glacial fjords. Some people call them sea parrots.

Beavers cut down trees and dam streams, which can cause flooding, but the ponds they create also provide important habitat for other species, from small fish and insects to birds and other mammals.

Beavers

Do you see that pond, so still and serene,
reflecting the trees all shimmering green
and the gentle clouds away up high,
scudding along in the summer sky?

We created that pond. It's just what we do.
When we hear running water, we react to the cue.
Beavers, you know, are not ones to shirk.
If there is a task, we are ready to work.

So we felled the trees and dragged them along
where the glacier's melt was racing strong.
We constructed a dam where the water rushed,
piling log after log, till the waters hushed.

We don't just build dams. See that shape like a dome?
That's the top of our lodge, the place we call home.
We selected a spot, just past glacier silt,
as the place we wanted our home to be built.

With logs, twigs, and shrubs, we made our lodge snug.
In the cracks, we used dirt, mud, and moss as a plug.
Insulating with mud keeps the place dry and warm,
this home where our kits—our babies—were born.

For two years we raised them, and when they were grown,
into the world, off they went, on their own.
They're now building dams on some other streams—
adult, healthy beavers, fulfilling their dreams.

Dragonflies

I shimmer in the air.
I buzz. I hum.
Look out mosquitoes,
here I come!
I hover. I swoop.
I strike. I eat.
Glacier mosquitoes
taste pretty sweet!

Alaska hosts about 30 species of dragonflies. The
four-spot skimmer is Alaska's state insect, chosen
by Alaska schoolchildren in 1995.

Wolves

I'm a creature of myth
and mystery.
The stories folks tell?
They'd scare even me.
Of course I'm wild.
I'm meant to be.

Do we howl at the moon?
No, that's not right.
We do howl more
when it's light at night,
which happens, of course,
when the moon shines bright.

We hunt—not for fun,
but to stay alive.
Food can be scarce.
We fight to survive.
We must be fierce
if our pack is to thrive.

What our kind needs
is no mystery.
Being ourselves
requires being free.
Yes, we are wild.
We're meant to be!

Wolves can go a week without food but can make up for it by gorging
on 20 pounds in a day, perhaps from a successful moose hunt.

Adult bald eagles have a wing span of six to seven feet. Bald eagles can be found in every state except Hawaii, but Alaska has the largest concentration in the United States.

Bald Eagles

This artist of the clouds
      brushes across the sky's canvas,
           hovers on streams of air—

swoops
      spiraling
         tumbling
            toying with the wind.

Freedom
      must surely
         look like this!

Porcupines

Look up! Look up!
Way up in the tree.
It isn't a nest.
What you're seeing is me!

I'm a wonderful climber.
People often don't know
that I'm up above
while they're walking below.

I've even been known
to sleep way up high—
a ball full of quills
'neath a blanket of sky.

My tail helps me climb.
It's muscled and strong.
Bristled hairs on the bottom
help my climbing along.

I'm best known because
of this fabulous feature:
the quills that make me
so splendid a creature.

Quills are specialized hairs
with barbs on their tips.
Bite me, you'll end up
with quills in your lips!

But I can't shoot my quills,
so you don't have to worry.
Just don't try to hug me.
I'm not a bit furry!

It is estimated that an adult porcupine has around 30,000 quills. Porcupines can be found throughout much of Alaska, from glacier trails to neighborhood streets and yards.

Ravens

Wind riders
    high gliders
        snow sliders.

Mischief makers
    garbage takers
        silence breakers.

Sideways walkers
    scratchy squawkers
        noisy talkers!

Ravens.

The sideways gait of ravens on the ground looks awkward, but they are acrobats in the air. They are also well-known scavengers, so don't leave food or garbage unattended!

Common Loons

The loon, the loon,
the remarkable loon.
I love that bird
and its warbling tune.
Whenever I hear it—
day, night, or noon—
I'm thrilled to the core
by the song of the loon.

The loon, the loon
that they call "common loon"—
I heard it one night,
as I watched a full moon,
and I've not been the same
since I first heard it croon
its razzling, dazzling,
mystical tune,
a gift of the wild
from this marvelous loon.

The loon, the loon,
that lovable loon
sings a trilling, a tremolo,
a yodeling tune.
A giggle, a quack,
a howl to the moon
are some of its calls, but
what makes me swoon
is its haunting, shivering,
trembling tune.
I'm in love, I'm in love
with the song of the loon.

Loons are sometimes known as "spirits of the wilderness."

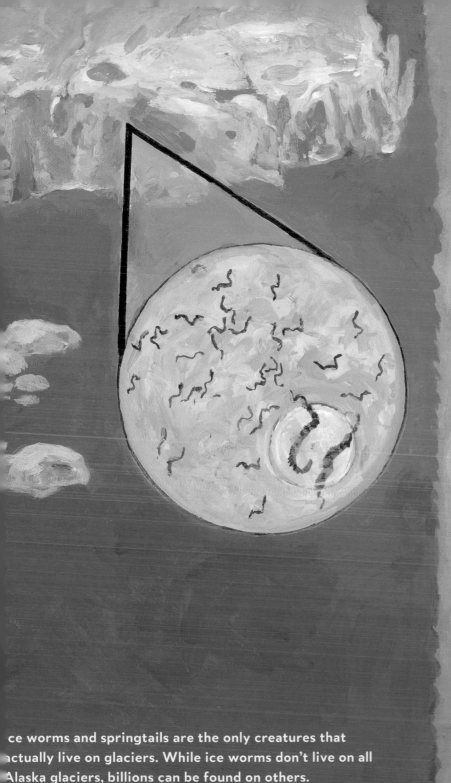

Ice worms and springtails are the only creatures that actually live on glaciers. While ice worms don't live on all Alaska glaciers, billions can be found on others.

Ice Worms

Fact 1: You might be surprised, but here's the deal:
Ice worms aren't a joke. They're real!

Fact 2: Photos of an ice worm's wiggles
look a lot like pencil scribbles.

Fact 3: These small, skinny worms can be black, brown, or blue,
and billions can live on one glacier—and do.

Fact 4: Ice worms are kin to earthworms and leeches,
but they aren't found in lakes, or dirt, or on beaches.

Fact 5: They are just found on glaciers in North America's west,
but only on some of those. What's with the rest?

Fact 6: Glacier temperature, some say, is one of the keys.
Too warm, they can't live, but too cold and they freeze.

Fact 7: They melt into a puddle if held in your hand—
not because they don't like you. It's heat they can't stand.

Fact 8: They hide deep in the glacier when the sunlight is bright,
then resurface for dinner when day turns to night.

Fact 9: They eat algae, bacteria, pollen grains too,
that they find in the snow and ice. Really. Who knew?

Fact 10: Bristles on their bodies help the worms grip.
As they travel the glacier, do they ever slip?

Fact 11: Slipping or not, ice worms show real power.
They can move on the glacier at ten feet per hour.

Fact 12: You can't carry ice worms back home in your pack,
but just knowing they're real is a pretty cool fact.

Humpback Whales

It bursts from the water,
lifts into the mists.
Unbelievable that such
a creature exists.

Forty tons of whale
rising into the space
between water and sky—
a moment of grace.

When the gasps, the whoops,
and applause start to lift,
you're left with the sense
you've been given a gift.

A humpback whale breaching
is hard to describe,
but the memory lingers.
You hold it inside.

And when you remember,
your smile is wide.

Humpback whales are baleen whales. Baleen is a flexible material
that hangs in strips from their upper jaws. The whales gulp water,
which the baleen filters out, trapping tiny fish and krill behind.

Red Squirrels

Look over here!
Look over there!
Red squirrels,
red squirrels
everywhere!
Up this tree.
Down that path.
Counting them
takes so much math!
Rush to a nest.
Off to the midden
where they keep
their spruce cones hidden.
Slip here.
Nip there.
Dash, scamper
everywhere.
Their hurry and scurry
make me dizzy!
Why are red squirrels
always busy?
Look over here!
Look over there!
Red squirrels,
red squirrels
everywhere!

While visitors collect memories to bring home, red squirrels are busily collecting spruce and other cones from dawn to dusk, food for the coming winter.

Plants

Plants taste
the slow dreams
of melting ice,
sink in the memory
of ancient times.
Mosses and ferns.
Salmonberries and spruce.
Devil's club, alder, willow.
We live here too!

How Are Glaciers Formed?

Glaciers begin to form when snow falls year after year and doesn't melt away during the summer months. As the buildup of snow gets thicker and heavier, the weight of the top layers presses down on the snow below, compacting it into dense ice. This takes years, but over time the ice becomes so heavy it begins to gradually move down toward sea level, pulled by its own weight, and becomes a glacier. As a result of this slow, flowing motion, glaciers are often called "rivers of ice."

Ice fields are vast interconnected glaciers, usually across a mountain range, their paths strongly influenced by the underlying landscape.

Valley glaciers are glaciers that spill down mountain valleys. Nabesna Glacier in Wrangell–St. Elias National Park and Preserve, near Copper Center, is the world's longest interior valley glacier. Matanuska Glacier, another valley glacier, is the largest glacier accessible by car in the United States. It is about 100 miles northeast of Anchorage.

When valley glaciers reach the sea, they are known as **tidewater glaciers**. Hubbard Glacier, near Yakutat, is the longest tidewater glacier in North America. Some glaciers are tidewater glaciers at high tide but otherwise don't reach the water. Lituya and Riggs Glaciers in Glacier Bay National Park and Preserve are among those.

VALLEY GLACIER

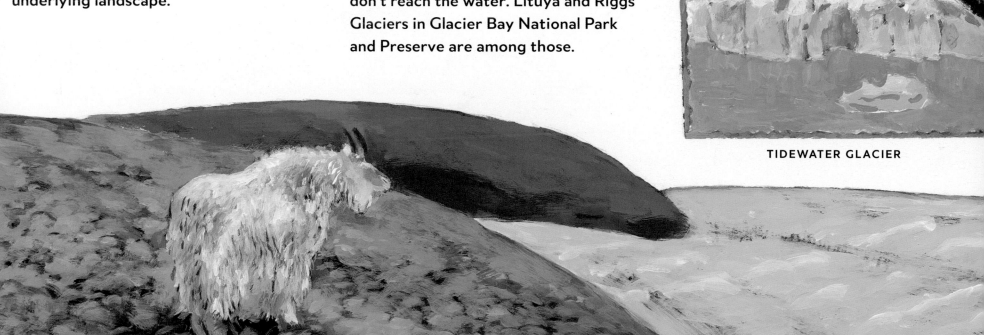

TIDEWATER GLACIER

PIEDMONT GLACIER

HANGING GLACIER

Piedmont glaciers occur when valley glaciers spill out into plains and spread out—like a large, icy fan. Malaspina Glacier, located primarily within Wrangell–St. Elias National Park and Preserve, is the largest piedmont glacier in the world. It is fed by ice streams from the St. Elias Range, with Seward Glacier being the principal feeder.

Hanging glaciers appear to be clinging to a mountain. They either originate high on the wall of a glacier valley—but do not descend far enough to connect to the surface of the main glacier—or they become disconnected when left behind as a major valley glacier system retreats and thins. Middle and Explorer Glaciers in the Chugach National Forest, south of Anchorage, are hanging glaciers.

All glaciers are continuously flowing downhill under the force of gravity. When more snow and ice build up on the glacier than melt away, glaciers extend farther down the valley and are described as advancing. A few Alaska glaciers are advancing, including Johns Hopkins and Hubbard Glaciers. However, about 95 percent of Alaska's glaciers are retreating, meaning that there isn't enough snow and ice building up to offset the snow and ice being lost to melting and evaporation. These retreating glaciers are getting shorter, ending higher and higher up their valleys, even though their ice is still flowing down. Students, scientists, and leaders around the world are paying attention to the effects of climate change, and glacier study is an important part of that effort.

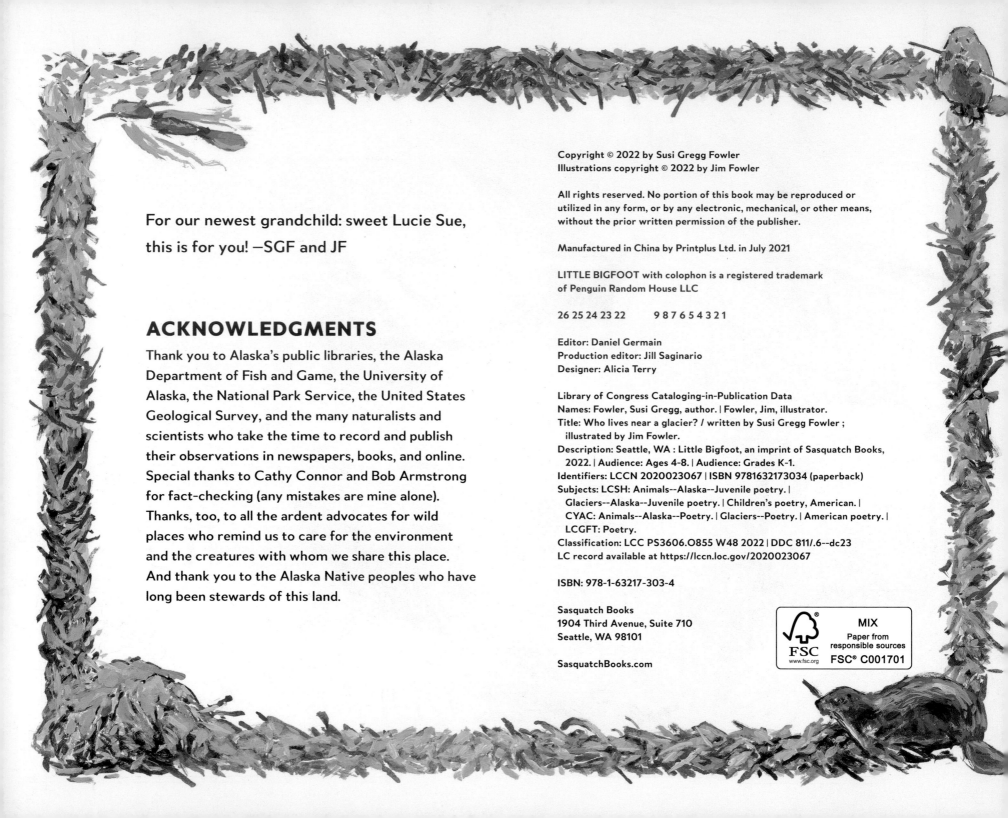

For our newest grandchild: sweet Lucie Sue,
this is for you! —SGF and JF

ACKNOWLEDGMENTS

Thank you to Alaska's public libraries, the Alaska
Department of Fish and Game, the University of
Alaska, the National Park Service, the United States
Geological Survey, and the many naturalists and
scientists who take the time to record and publish
their observations in newspapers, books, and online.
Special thanks to Cathy Connor and Bob Armstrong
for fact-checking (any mistakes are mine alone).
Thanks, too, to all the ardent advocates for wild
places who remind us to care for the environment
and the creatures with whom we share this place.
And thank you to the Alaska Native peoples who have
long been stewards of this land.

Manufactured in China by Printplus Ltd. in July 2021

LITTLE BIGFOOT with colophon is a registered trademark
of Penguin Random House LLC

26 25 24 23 22   9 8 7 6 5 4 3 2 1

Editor: Daniel Germain
Production editor: Jill Saginario
Designer: Alicia Terry

Library of Congress Cataloging-in-Publication Data
Names: Fowler, Susi Gregg, author. | Fowler, Jim, illustrator.
Title: Who lives near a glacier? / written by Susi Gregg Fowler ;
 illustrated by Jim Fowler.
Description: Seattle, WA : Little Bigfoot, an imprint of Sasquatch Books,
 2022. | Audience: Ages 4-8. | Audience: Grades K-1.
Identifiers: LCCN 2020023067 | ISBN 9781632173034 (paperback)
Subjects: LCSH: Animals--Alaska--Juvenile poetry. |
 Glaciers--Alaska--Juvenile poetry. | Children's poetry, American. |
 CYAC: Animals--Alaska--Poetry. | Glaciers--Poetry. | American poetry. |
 LCGFT: Poetry.
Classification: LCC PS3606.O855 W48 2022 | DDC 811/.6--dc23
LC record available at https://lccn.loc.gov/2020023067

ISBN: 978-1-63217-303-4

Sasquatch Books
1904 Third Avenue, Suite 710
Seattle, WA 98101

SasquatchBooks.com

FSC
www.fsc.org

MIX
Paper from
responsible sources
FSC® C001701